HEALTHY SMOOTHIES

GOOD HOUSEKEEPING

HEALTHY SMOOTHIES

60 ENERGIZING BLENDER DRINKS & MORE!

★ GOOD FOOD GUARANTEED ★

HEARSTBOOKS

HEARSTBOOKS

An Imprint of Sterling Publishing
1166 Avenue of the Americas
New York, NY 10036

ISBN 978-1-61837-215-4

GOOD HOUSEKEEPING
Jane Francisco
EDITOR IN CHIEF
Melissa Geurts
DESIGN DIRECTOR
Susan Westmoreland
FOOD DIRECTOR
Sharon Franke
FOOD APPLIANCES DIRECTOR

The Good Housekeeping Cookbook Seal guarantees that the recipes in this cookbook meet
the strict standards of the Good Housekeeping Research Institute. The Institute has been a source of
reliable information and a consumer advocate since 1900, and established its seal of approval in 1909.
Every recipe has been triple-tested for ease, reliability, and great taste.

Distributed in Canada by Sterling Publishing
c/o Canadian Manda Group, 664 Annette Street
Toronto, Ontario, Canada M6S 2C8
Distributed in Australia by Capricorn Link (Australia) Pty. Ltd.
P.O. Box 704, Windsor, NSW 2756, Australia

www.goodhousekeeping.com

For information about custom editions, special sales, and premium and corporate purchases,
please contact Sterling Special Sales at 800-805-5489 or specialsales@sterlingpublishing.com.

Cover Design: Scott Russo
Interior Design: Barbara Balch
Project Editor: Carol Prager

Manufactured in China

2 4 6 8 10 9 7 5 3 1

www.sterlingpublishing.com

CONTENTS

Berry Batido
(page 66)

Foreword

Good Housekeeping's first coverage of smoothies was in a book called *Blend It!* It featured all sorts of recipes to make in—you guessed it—a blender. Lots of delicious stuff from pancake batter to pesto to pina coladas. We've come a long way. These days I find myself using the blender more often but for less caloric options. Yes, smoothies and puréed juices are available almost everywhere, though some are healthier than others, and some are quite expensive. Enter *Good Housekeeping Healthy Smoothies*. Here you'll find some of the test kitchen's favorite morning starters, afternoon pick-me-ups and a batch of delicious soups to buzz when a more savory craving strikes.

    Not all smoothies are created equal. Some days I want the bright straight-up jolt of Greens in a Glass, other days I need the creamy satisfaction of a Java Banana Smoothie. Consider starting your day with a Sunrise or Strawberry-Chia Smoothie. Avocado in a smoothie, you bet—it lends a silkiness that you'll love and a smidge of healthy fat that'll keep you satisfied long into the morning. Use these recipes as a jumping off point to create even more favorites. All you've got to do is Blend It!

SUSAN WESTMORELAND
Food Director, *Good Housekeeping*

Introduction

There's no question smoothies deserve some serious respect. One: they're ready in a flash for breakfast, as a snack, or a treat. Two: they can be a nutritional powerhouse—full of antioxidants, minerals, vitamins, and protein. And three: they're a great way to increase your daily servings of fruits and vegetables. Sounds simple enough. But ready-made smoothies from grocery stores and quick-service chains can clock in at 400 calories for a 20-ounce cup. So depending on their ingredients, smoothies can quickly turn into unhealthy calorie-bombs filled with sugar and saturated fat.

That's where *Good Housekeeping Healthy Smoothies* comes in. With fabulous recipes and must-have tips, we'll get your liquid groove going in the right direction. Better yet, our collection includes not just healthy smoothies, but also guilt-free refreshing sippers like classic fruit blends, brisk tea, and fizzy concoctions. We even put your blender to work preparing eight outstanding healthy soups.

How to Make a Healthy Smoothie

To ensure your blend is both delicious and nutritious, follow these simple smoothie tips:

1 **Follow Recipe Directions.** It's tempting to think of a smoothie as a little of this and that. But this carefree method is destined for trouble, adding calories, sugar, and fat to your drink. By measuring ingredients according to our directions, you'll keep the nutrition stats in check, while also ensuring a good solid-to-liquid ratio.

2 **Be Liquid Savvy.** The liquid component of a smoothie is essential—it's what helps the ingredients blend with ease. If using fruit juice, make sure it's 100 percent unsweetened. Plain low-fat yogurt gives your smoothie a healthy dose of filling protein without excess calories, while almond milk and light coconut milk add a hit of rich flavor and creamy texture.

3 **Go Fresh (If You Can).** The fresher the juice and ingredients you use in your smoothie, the better the flavor and nutrition. Use organic ingredients whenever possible, not only to increase nutrition and avoid pesticides, but also for better taste.

4 **Don't Underestimate Ice.** It's the best way to thicken a frosty smoothie without adding calories.

5 **Stick to One Serving.** If you're using a smoothie as a meal replacement, it's natural to think you'll need a larger portion. But even if you're only adding more fruit, the calories and sugar can creep up quickly. Smoothies that are high in fiber, like recipes with oats (see Berry Satisfying Smoothie, page 17) or avocado (see Healthy Banana Milkshake, page 40), will make you feel fuller longer.

6 **Get Creative.** Once you've mastered a recipe or two, try adding different flavors, like a spoonful of unsweetened cocoa powder, a pinch of cinnamon or freshly grated nutmeg, or even a shot of hot pepper sauce.

Frozen Assets

Frozen fruit is a smoothie's BFF.

For a lusciously thick smoothie, using a creamy fruit like mango, banana, or avocado is a good move. However, frozen fruit will make your healthy smoothie even creamier. This is especially true with summer fruit: freezing is a great way to preserve their color, flavor, and nutrient value. (Plus they're a great sub for ice cubes.)

BERRY PICKING POINTERS

- Berries should be plump, fresh-looking, and uniformly colored.
- Avoid crushed or bruised fruit and cartons stained with juice.
- Beware of fuzzy fruit—mold spreads quickly from berry to berry.

PREFREEZING PREP

- **STRAWBERRIES:** Rinse, drain, then hull; halve or quarter if you like.
- **RASPBERRIES:** Remove stems or leaves. Rinse carefully; drain.
- **BLUEBERRIES:** Remove stems and freeze unrinsed. Quickly rinse under cold water just before using.
- **BLACKBERRIES:** Remove stems or leaves. Rinse carefully; drain.
- **PEACHES, APRICOTS, NECTARINES, AND PLUMS:** Remove pits; cut into halves or wedges and toss with a bit of lemon juice to prevent browning.
- **BANANAS:** Peel and break into small chunks.

CHILL OUT

- Arrange fruit in a single layer, without touching, on a jelly-roll pan lined with parchment paper.
- Freeze, uncovered, until hard, about four hours.
- Transfer fruit to freezer-weight bags (the quart size is great for single-serving portions), press out excess air, lay flat, and freeze up to six months.

Healthy Smoothie Additions

Different superfoods not only boost the nutrition of your smoothie, they can increase your taste and texture experience. Here are our faves:

- **CHIA SEEDS** These tiny wonders can hold up to 9 times their weight in liquid, which makes their ability to form a gel a perfect way to thicken a smoothie. Chia seeds expand in your stomach, keeping you fuller for longer; plus, their high protein and fiber content boost satiety. Prior to blending, soak the seeds in a little water to give your smoothie a nice smooth consistency. *Add 1 tablespoon per serving.*

- **GROUND FLAXSEEDS** This all-star seed contains both the insoluble and soluble fibers important for gastrointestinal health, as well as for reducing cholesterol levels. Flax gives you a protein boost; plus it's high in omega-3s, a good fat shown to have heart-healthy effects and reduce inflammation, thereby cutting the risk of diabetes. *Add 1 tablespoon per serving.*

- **ALMOND, CASHEW, AND PEANUT BUTTER** These are a good source of heart-healthy unsaturated fats, protein, and fiber. Nut butter also helps provide long-lasting energy. *Add 1 tablespoon per serving.*

- **OATS AND OAT BRAN** Rich in soluble fiber, which can help slash cholesterol levels and stabilize blood sugar, this grain is also mild in taste, so it blends well with other ingredients. Oats may also increase appetite control hormones, leaving you feeling fuller longer. *Add 1 tablespoon per serving.*

A WORD ABOUT SWEETNESS

To make our smoothies the healthiest they can be, we're extra stingy with the sugar, leaving fruit and sweeter veggies (hello carrots and beets!) to do the job. However, if you want your smoothie a little sweeter, there are more healthful choices:

- **DATES** For best results, remove the pits and soak them overnight or for at least an hour before blending.
- **HONEY OR MAPLE SYRUP** Since both ingredients are sweeter than the white stuff, add sparingly.
- **APPLE, BANANA, OR PINEAPPLE** A chunk or two of these naturally sweet fruits works wonders in a winter smoothie or if your other fruits aren't perfectly ripe.
- **VANILLA OR ALMOND EXTRACT** Just a drop adds a burst of intense sweetness. Use pure (versus imitation flavor) for best results.

BLENDER SMARTS

Whether you're whipping up a healthy smoothie or one of our fabulous soups, follow these five essential rules so your blender can work its very best.

1 **Treat liquids and solids equally.** Place liquid ingredients in the jar first, followed by the rest of the ingredients. The vortex created by blending the liquids will pull the solids down, making sure you get an even blend.

2 **Let hot liquids breathe.** When blending a hot mixture for a soup, remove the filler cap from the cover to reduce steam buildup and avoid spurting.

3 **Don't forget the "Pulse" button.** Have some food stuck under the blade? Use the "Pulse" feature to dislodge it.

4 **Mix it up.** For the best results, stop the machine and stir occasionally.

5 **Clean your blender efficiently.** To clear seeds and dried gunk out of your machine, fill the jar halfway with water and add a drop of liquid dishwashing detergent. Blend for a few seconds. Be sure to rinse thoroughly in the sink.

Banana-Berry Blast Smoothie
(page 14)

1 Breakfast Blends

If your morning means a whirl of grab-and-go breakfasts, count on a built-for-speed smoothie to bring nutritious and delicious together. Try our Banana-Berry Blast or Berry Satisfying Smoothie—they're sure family favorites. Or treat yourself to a Strawberry-Chia Smoothie or Mocha Blast Smoothie. Plan ahead: Fill your blender bowl with the smoothie ingredients (except for ice and frozen fruit), cover tightly, and stash in the fridge overnight. Then wake up, push a button, and presto! Breakfast is ready!

Banana-Berry Blast
SMOOTHIE

Get your morning off to a "berry" good start
with this tasty blend of fresh blueberries and your pick
of raspberries or blackberries. For photo, see page 12.

TOTAL TIME: 5 MINUTES   **MAKES:** 2 SERVINGS (ABOUT 3¼ CUPS)

1   small ripe banana, cut up

¾   cup pineapple-orange juice

½   cup ice cubes

1   container (6 ounces) blueberries

1   container (6 ounces) raspberries or blackberries

2   teaspoons honey

1   teaspoon grated, peeled fresh ginger

In blender, combine banana, pineapple-orange juice, ice, blueberries, raspberries, honey, and ginger and blend until mixture is smooth and frothy. Pour into 2 tall glasses.

EACH SERVING: ABOUT 205 CALORIES, 3G PROTEIN, 51G CARBOHYDRATE, 1G TOTAL FAT (0G SATURATED), 9G FIBER, 0MG CHOLESTEROL, 8MG SODIUM.

TIP

The freshest blueberries should have a soft, hazy white coating, called "bloom." Bloom is a completely natural part of blueberries that helps protect the fruit from harsh sunlight.

Berry Beneficial

These summer beauties are seriously good for you.

Berries are true health stars. Antioxidant-rich with body-wide benefits, their calorie cost is low: One cup of raspberries, for example, has only 65 calories and no fat (plus a healthy 8 grams of fiber). So you can fill your blender with berries this morning—without the guilt.

DISCOVER BLACKBERRIES

They have the most antioxidants per serving—even more than superfoods like red wine, dark chocolate, or red cabbage.

BUZZ UP SOME VITAMIN C

One serving of strawberries (about one cup) contains 144 percent of the daily value of C. That's 24 percent more than a typical 8-ounce glass of OJ from a carton. Plus, a cup of strawberries has about as much fiber (4 grams) as 2 slices of whole wheat bread.

BENEFIT FROM THE BLUES

Research suggests blueberries may help keep high blood pressure in check. Canadian researchers report that feeding stroke-prone animals a blueberry-enriched diet for six weeks lowered their systolic blood pressure (the top number) by 30 percent, compared with that of animals on a control diet.

Berry Satisfying Smoothie

Jump-Start SMOOTHIE

Spiked with fresh ginger, this smoothie has just the right *oomph*
to get your morning off to a delicious start.

TOTAL TIME: 5 MINUTES   MAKES: 2 SERVINGS

1   cup frozen strawberries

½   cup fresh blueberries

½   cup orange-tangerine juice blend, chilled

2   teaspoons chopped, peeled fresh ginger

¼   cup plain low-fat yogurt

2   ice cubes

In blender, combine strawberries, blueberries,
orange-tangerine juice, ginger, yogurt, and
ice. Blend until mixture is smooth and frothy,
scraping down side of container occasionally.
Pour into 2 tall glasses.

EACH SERVING: ABOUT 96 CALORIES, 3G PROTEIN,
21G CARBOHYDRATE, 1G TOTAL FAT (0G SATURATED),
2G FIBER, 2MG CHOLESTEROL, 24MG SODIUM.

Berry Satisfying SMOOTHIE

Add fiber-rich oats to a morning smoothie? Absolutely!
It makes it extra filling.

TOTAL TIME: 5 MINUTES   MAKES: 4 SERVINGS

2   cups frozen mixed berries

1   cup vanilla low-fat yogurt

1   ripe banana, sliced

½   cup quick-cooking oats

½   cup orange juice

4   teaspoons honey

In blender, combine mixed berries, yogurt,
banana, oats, orange juice, and honey and blend
until mixture is smooth and frothy. Pour into 4
glasses.

EACH SERVING: ABOUT 185 CALORIES, 6G PROTEIN,
40G CARBOHYDRATE, 2G TOTAL FAT (0G SATURATED),
4G FIBER, 3MG CHOLESTEROL, 41MG SODIUM.

Strawberry & Apricot
SMOOTHIE

For a protein boost, add a spoonful of toasted sliced almonds
to this morning blend.

TOTAL TIME: 5 MINUTES   **MAKES:** 2 SERVINGS

1   cup fresh or frozen strawberries

1   cup unsweetened apricot juice, chilled

½   cup plain low-fat yogurt

4   ice cubes (if using fresh fruit)

In blender, combine strawberries, apricot juice, yogurt, and ice (if using) and blend until mixture is smooth and frothy. Pour into 2 glasses.

EACH SERVING: ABOUT 130 CALORIES, 4G PROTEIN, 27G CARBOHYDRATE, 1G TOTAL FAT (0G SATURATED), 2G FIBER, 4MG CHOLESTEROL, 51MG SODIUM.

TIP

Buy the largest bag of supermarket-brand frozen unsweetened strawberries you can find. Not only are they a major bargain for this recipe, you can stash the extras to whirl up more morning smoothies. The berries are individually frozen, so you can measure whatever amount you need.

Strawberry-Chia
SMOOTHIE

OJ isn't the only way to get your vitamin C in the morning.
Kiwis and strawberries are also a good source, and this fruity blend
with crunchy chia seeds is custom-made to rev up your day.

TOTAL TIME: 10 MINUTES   **MAKES:** 1 SERVING

1 cup frozen strawberries

2 kiwifruit, peeled and chopped

3/4 cup fat-free milk

1 tablespoon chia seeds

1 teaspoon ground ginger

4 ice cubes

In blender, combine strawberries, kiwifruit, milk, chia seeds, ginger, and ice and blend until smooth and frothy. Pour into 1 tall glass.

EACH SERVING: ABOUT 256 CALORIES, 10G PROTEIN, 49G CARBOHYDRATE, 4G TOTAL FAT (1G SATURATED), 11G FIBER, 4MG CHOLESTEROL, 86MG SODIUM.

TIP

When purchasing chia seeds, take note of the use-by date on the package. If buying in bulk, store the seeds in an airtight container in a cool, dry place for up to several months.

Peach-Almond
SMOOTHIE

Ripe peaches are a must for this smoothie.
But there's wiggle room when choosing: from firm-ripe fruit (with slight give when pressed), to those with more give, to those that are soft and ready to eat. Their background color (near the stem end) should have a yellow, amber, or golden hue, not a greenish tinge.

ACTIVE TIME: 15 MINUTES   **TOTAL TIME:** 20 MINUTES
MAKES: 2¾ SERVINGS

1   cup peeled, sliced peaches (about 2 medium)

1   cup unsweetened peach juice

½   cup vanilla low-fat yogurt

1 to 2 drops almond extract

3   ice cubes

In blender, combine peaches, peach juice, yogurt, almond extract, and ice and blend until smooth and frothy. Pour into 2 tall glasses.

EACH SERVING: ABOUT 143 CALORIES, 4G PROTEIN, 32G CARBOHYDRATE, 1G TOTAL FAT (0G SATURATED), 1G FIBER, 3MG CHOLESTEROL, 48MG SODIUM.

TIP

Another benefit for using ripe peaches in this recipe (aside from fabulous flavor)? You can easily peel them with a serrated peeler.

Banana-Peanut Butter
SMOOTHIE

For a skinnier but equally protein-friendly smoothie,
skip the peanut butter and swap in 2 teaspoons peanut butter powder
mixed with 1 teaspoon water.

TOTAL TIME: 10 MINUTES   **MAKES:** 1 SERVING (ABOUT 1½ CUPS)

1   small ripe banana, cut in half

½   cup low-fat (1%) milk

1   teaspoon creamy peanut butter

1   teaspoon honey, optional

3   ice cubes

In blender, combine banana, milk, peanut butter, honey (if using), and ice and blend until mixture is smooth and frothy. Pour into 1 tall glass.

EACH SERVING: ABOUT 165 CALORIES, 6G PROTEIN, 28G CARBOHYDRATE, 4G TOTAL FAT (2G SATURATED), 2G FIBER, 5MG CHOLESTEROL, 85MG SODIUM.

TIP

Stuck with a bunch of unripe bananas? Plan ahead and flash-ripen them in the freezer! The fruit will turn black and fully ripe in a few hours. (Your smoothies will be colder and thicker, too.)

Double Orange Smoothie

Double Orange SMOOTHIE

Orange juice and DIY frozen orange sections
give this morning marvel its double dose of citrus.

TOTAL TIME: 10 MINUTES PLUS FREEZING **MAKES:** 2 SERVINGS

1   navel orange, peeled

1   cup vanilla low-fat yogurt

1   cup ice cubes

½   cup orange juice

2   teaspoons honey

1 Cut orange into sections; transfer sections to small freezer container. Cover and freeze until sections are frozen solid.

2 In blender, combine yogurt, ice, orange juice, honey, and frozen orange sections and blend until smooth and frothy. Pour into 2 glasses.

EACH SERVING: ABOUT 188 CALORIES, 7G PROTEIN, 37G CARBOHYDRATE, 2G TOTAL FAT (1G SATURATED), 2G FIBER, 6MG CHOLESTEROL, 82MG SODIUM.

TIP

This smoothie is divine when prepared with a blood orange. Available January through April, its intense orange flavor with a hint of raspberry will make this recipe shine.

Rise & Shine SMOOTHIE

The nutrient-rich powerhouse wheat germ offers a significant dose
of vitamins, minerals, and protein, and gives this pineapple-kissed
smoothie a burst of nutty flavor and toothsome crunch.

TOTAL TIME: 5 MINUTES **MAKES:** 4 SERVINGS

1   large ripe banana

2   cups frozen pineapple chunks

2   cups ice cubes

1   cup orange juice

½   cup vanilla low-fat yogurt

¼   cup wheat germ

In blender, combine banana, pineapple, ice, orange juice, yogurt, and wheat germ and blend until mixture is smooth and frothy. Pour into 4 glasses.

EACH SERVING: ABOUT 158 CALORIES, 5G PROTEIN, 34G CARBOHYDRATE, 1G TOTAL FAT (0G SATURATED), 3G FIBER, 2MG CHOLESTEROL, 21MG SODIUM.

BREAKFAST BLENDS

Pomegranate-Berry
SMOOTHIE

High in vitamin C and potassium, a great source of fiber, and low in calories, the pomegranate definitely earns its power-food status. Now readily available as unsweetened juice, its rich, tangy taste pairs beautifully with mixed berries in this thick and creamy smoothie.

TOTAL TIME: 5 MINUTES   **MAKES:** 1 SERVING (ABOUT 1²/₃ CUPS)

½   cup pomegranate juice, chilled

½   cup vanilla low-fat yogurt

1   cup frozen mixed berries

In blender, combine pomegranate juice, yogurt, and berries and blend until mixture is smooth and frothy. Pour into 1 tall glass.

EACH SERVING: ABOUT 250 CALORIES, 6G PROTEIN, 52G CARBOHYDRATE, 2G TOTAL FAT (1G SATURATED), 5G FIBER, 8MG CHOLESTEROL, 110MG SODIUM.

TIP

Frozen mixed berries typically include strawberries, blueberries, raspberries, and blackberries, but that doesn't mean you can't concoct your own gourmet blend. Try a 1-cup mix of frozen dark sweet cherries, raspberries, and blueberries.

Mocha Blast
SMOOTHIE

This blender breakfast gives you a beauty boost while powering you through a hectic morning. Cocoa powder provides skin-protecting flavonols, and almond butter delivers healthy fats to support supple skin.

TOTAL TIME: 5 MINUTES   **MAKES:** 1 SERVING

1   ripe banana, cut into pieces

1   cup ice cubes

½   cup fat-free vanilla Greek yogurt

¼   cup cold-brewed coffee (see Perfect Cold-Brewed Coffee, page 39)

1   teaspoon almond butter

2   teaspoons unsweetened cocoa

½   teaspoon vanilla extract

sugar, optional

In blender, combine banana, ice, yogurt, coffee, almond butter, cocoa powder, and vanilla and blend until mixture is smooth and frothy. Add sugar to taste, if using. Pour into 1 tall glass.

EACH SERVING: ABOUT 252 CALORIES, 12G PROTEIN, 45G CARBOHYDRATE, 4G TOTAL FAT (1G SATURATED), 5G FIBER, 0MG CHOLESTEROL, 48MG SODIUM.

TIP

This recipe is equally delish with cashew butter.

Protein Power Smoothie
(page 32)

2 | Power Up

Move over, coffee. These protein-rich smoothies will provide you with an instant lift that lasts. You'll find tangy yogurt in our Calcium Boost Smoothie and Frosty Berry-Apple Smoothie to keep you energized post-workout. And with almond butter in the mix, our Healthy Banana Milkshake and Cocoa-Almond Smoothie will provide just the *oomph* you need to soar through the afternoon. If you prefer your protein fix without the dairy, any of our recipes can be made with almond or soy milk.

Protein Power
SMOOTHIE

This fruity smoothie delivers a serious protein boost,
thanks to vanilla whey protein powder. For photo, see page 30.

TOTAL TIME: 5 MINUTES   **MAKES:** 1 SERVING

¾ cup fat-free milk

½ ripe banana

½ cup frozen raspberries

½ cup frozen blueberries

1 scoop (1 ounce) vanilla whey protein powder

5 ice cubes

In blender, combine milk, banana, raspberries, blueberries, protein powder, and ice and blend until mixture is smooth and frothy. Pour into 1 tall glass.

EACH SERVING: ABOUT 284 CALORIES, 25G PROTEIN, 44G CARBOHYDRATE, 2G TOTAL FAT (1G SATURATED), 6G FIBER, 39MG CHOLESTEROL, 118MG SODIUM.

Powder Boost

Make protein powder a go-to for extra energy.

Almost everyone can get enough protein through foods (healthy adults should get about 45 to 56 grams a day), but if you exercise regularly, you may want some extra protein now and then. Smoothies are a go-to for that, especially when you add a scoop of protein powder.

Shop for powders with single ingredients (look for "protein isolate" on the label) versus protein "shakes." Then choose from the following varieties (all are interchangeable in our recipes):

- **Whey protein powder** is a good choice, but it comes from milk, so make sure you can tolerate dairy.

- **Soy protein powder** is a plant-based protein. As effective as most animal sources of protein, it's also rich in nutrients.

- **Pea protein powder** is ideal for vegans, vegetarians, or those with sensitivities to dairy, eggs, or soy.

Calcium Boost
SMOOTHIE

Calcium-fortified orange juice and plain yogurt
are the dynamic duo in this snack-a-licious smoothie
sweetened with strawberries and a touch of honey.

TOTAL TIME: 5 MINUTES **MAKES:** 1 SERVING

1   cup frozen strawberries

1   container (6 ounces) plain fat-free yogurt

½   cup calcium-fortified orange juice

1   teaspoon honey

In blender, combine strawberries, yogurt, orange juice, and honey and blend until mixture is smooth and frothy. Pour into 1 tall glass.

EACH SERVING: ABOUT 227 CALORIES, 11G PROTEIN, 46G CARBOHYDRATE, 1G TOTAL FAT (0G SATURATED), 4G FIBER, 3MG CHOLESTEROL, 137MG SODIUM.

TIP

Add a spoonful of instant nonfat dry milk powder for even more calcium!

Frosty Berry-Apple
SMOOTHIE

Apple juice and a touch of honey give this smoothie
a lovely harvest taste.

TOTAL TIME: 5 MINUTES   **MAKES:** 1 SERVING

1   cup frozen mixed berries

½   cup unsweetened apple juice

½   cup plain low-fat yogurt

1   teaspoon honey

In blender, combine berries, apple juice, yogurt, and honey and blend until mixture is smooth and frothy. Pour into 1 tall glass.

EACH SERVING: ABOUT 215 CALORIES, 8G PROTEIN, 45G CARBOHYDRATE, 3G TOTAL FAT (1G SATURATED), 4G FIBER, 7MG CHOLESTEROL, 91MG SODIUM.

 TIP

Use fresh, unpasteurized apple cider from the farmers' market for an even more robust and earthy apple flavor.

Mighty Veggie
SMOOTHIE

Don't let the name throw you! This fabulous blend
of supersweet beets, carrots, orange juice, and frozen bananas
is a delicious way to power up—and get your veggies.

TOTAL TIME: 5 MINUTES   **MAKES:** 2 SERVINGS

4   small refrigerated cooked beets, sliced

3/4   cup shredded carrots

1   cup orange juice

2   frozen ripe bananas, cut up

1   tablespoon ground flaxseeds

In blender, combine beets, carrots, orange juice, bananas, and flaxseeds and blend until mixture is smooth and frothy. Pour into 2 glasses.

EACH SERVING: ABOUT 232 CALORIES, 5G PROTEIN, 53G CARBOHYDRATE, 2G TOTAL FAT (0G SATURATED), 7G FIBER, 0MG CHOLESTEROL, 94MG SODIUM.

TIP

Get even more veggies by using an unsweetened fruit and vegetable juice blend instead of plain OJ. You'll find it in the refrigerated juice section at the supermarket.

Java Banana
SMOOTHIE

Here's a frosty glass of Joe with a bonus: 1 banana per serving. Potassium-rich bananas not only stimulate your muscles, nerves, and brain cells, they can also help reduce blood pressure and risk of stroke.

TOTAL TIME: 5 MINUTES   **MAKES:** 2 SERVINGS

2   ripe bananas (preferably frozen), cut up

3/4   cup cold-brewed coffee
(see Perfect Cold-Brewed Coffee, right)

3/4   cup low-fat (1%) milk

2   teaspoons brown sugar

1   cup ice cubes

In blender, combine bananas, coffee, milk, brown sugar, and ice and blend until mixture is smooth and frothy. Pour into 2 glasses.

EACH SERVING: ABOUT 162 CALORIES, 4G PROTEIN, 36G CARBOHYDRATE, 1G TOTAL FAT (1G SATURATED), 3G FIBER, 5MG CHOLESTEROL, 44MG SODIUM.

Perfect
Cold-Brewed Coffee

Making authentic cold-brewed coffee (aka: iced coffee when served over ice) for smoothies couldn't be easier—or tastier. Cold brewing reduces the acidity of coffee, which in turn enhances its sweetness and other complex flavor notes. Here's how:

1   In a small pitcher or 1-quart measuring cup, whisk together ⅓ cup ground coffee and 1⅓ cups cold water until all the lumps are gone.

2   Cover tightly and refrigerate for at least 5 hours, but it's best left overnight (not much longer or it'll get bitter).

3   Strain the coffee through a coffee filter-lined strainer, pushing it through with a spatula. Makes ¾ cup.

COFFEE ICE CUBES

Double the recipe, left. Pour cold-brewed coffee into an ice-cube tray and freeze until solid. Place frozen cubes in a large freezer-weight bag, press out excess air, and freeze up to two weeks.

Healthy Banana
MILKSHAKE

Good-for-you avocado makes this smoothie
delectably thick and creamy.

TOTAL TIME: 5 MINUTES   **MAKES:** 2 SERVINGS

½ avocado

1 frozen ripe banana, chopped

1 cup unsweetened almond milk

1 teaspoon almond butter

1 teaspoon vanilla extract

In blender, combine avocado, banana, almond milk, almond butter, and vanilla and blend until mixture is smooth and frothy. Pour into 2 glasses.

EACH SERVING: ABOUT 175 CALORIES, 3G PROTEIN, 20G CARBOHYDRATE, 11G TOTAL FAT (1G SATURATED), 6G FIBER, 0MG CHOLESTEROL, 100MG SODIUM.

Go for the Gold!

Bananas are a potassium powerhouse.

A banana gives you more than great taste in your smoothie. For a measly 100 fat-free calories, a medium one (4 ounces without the peel) delivers about 450 milligrams of potassium. And according to the National Heart, Lung, and Blood Institute of the National Institutes of Health, a high intake of this mineral may stave off high blood pressure and improve blood pressure control in people who already have hypertension.

Strawberry-Date
SMOOTHIE

Dates are nutrient-dense in fiber, potassium, and manganese.
Better yet, because dates produce their caramel-like flavor naturally,
no added sugar is required when you add them to smoothies.

TOTAL TIME: 5 MINUTES   **MAKES:** 2 SERVINGS

1   cup unsweetened almond milk

8   ice cubes

6   frozen strawberries

3   pitted dates

¼   teaspoon vanilla extract

pinch salt

In blender, combine almond milk, ice, strawberries, dates, vanilla, and salt and blend until mixture is smooth and frothy. Pour into 1 tall glass.

EACH SERVING: ABOUT 116 CALORIES, 1G PROTEIN, 27G CARBOHYDRATE, 1G TOTAL FAT (0G SATURATED), 3G FIBER, 0MG CHOLESTEROL, 157MG SODIUM.

 TIP

If you like, use unsweetened soy milk instead of almond milk and swap in 2 dried figs for the dates in this recipe.

POWER UP

Strawberries & Cream
SMOOTHIE

Frozen peach slices and a small scoop of frozen yogurt
make this smoothie extra thick (and a tad decadent).
Whirl in 2 tablespoons of toasted wheat bran for a protein boost.

TOTAL TIME: 10 MINUTES   **MAKES:** 2 SERVINGS

1   pound strawberries, hulled

1   cup frozen peach slices

¼   cup vanilla low-fat frozen yogurt

¼   cup fat-free milk

2   teaspoons honey

In blender, combine strawberries, peach slices, frozen yogurt, milk, and honey and blend until mixture is smooth and frothy. Pour into 2 glasses.

EACH SERVING: ABOUT 175 CALORIES, 5G PROTEIN, 38G CARBOHYDRATE, 2G TOTAL FAT (1G SATURATED), 5G FIBER, 17MG CHOLESTEROL, 29MG SODIUM.

TIP

When in season, buy an extra 1-pound container of strawberries for another batch of these creamy smoothies later in the week. Arrange the berries (without washing or stemming) on a paper towel-lined tray, cover with plastic wrap, and refrigerate. Before using, wash under cool water and then remove the stems. (This will prevent the berries from turning moldy.)

Cocoa-Almond
SMOOTHIE

What's so brilliant about cocoa? It's a good source of iron, magnesium, and zinc, and clocks in at almost 2 grams of fiber per tablespoon. But most importantly, cocoa delivers maximum chocolate buzz without a trace of fat.

TOTAL TIME: 5 MINUTES   **MAKES:** 2 SERVINGS

2   ripe bananas (preferably frozen), cut up

3   pitted dates

2   tablespoons unsweetened cocoa

3/4   cup almond milk

2   teaspoons almond butter

1   cup ice cubes

In blender, combine bananas, dates, cocoa, almond milk, almond butter, and ice and blend until mixture is smooth and frothy. Pour into 2 glasses.

EACH SERVING: ABOUT 248 CALORIES, 5G PROTEIN, 55G CARBOHYDRATE, 5G TOTAL FAT (1G SATURATED), 8G FIBER, 0MG CHOLESTEROL, 89MG SODIUM.

TIP

Pump up the protein by adding an ounce or two of diced low-fat tofu to the mix.

Carrot-Coconut
SMOOTHIE

This energizing smoothie will remind you of carrot cake—
but without the guilt!

TOTAL TIME: 5 MINUTES   **MAKES:** 1 SERVING

1   cup freshly grated peeled carrots

1   cup frozen pineapple chunks

1   small apple, peeled and diced

¼   cup light coconut milk

pinch ground cinnamon

In blender, combine carrots, pineapple, apple, coconut milk, and cinnamon and blend until mixture is smooth and frothy. Pour into 1 glass.

EACH SERVING: ABOUT 242 CALORIES, 4G PROTEIN, 53G CARBOHYDRATE, 5G TOTAL FAT (3G SATURATED), 8G FIBER, 0MG CHOLESTEROL, 81MG SODIUM.

TIP

Indulge yourself by choosing a sweet apple like Golden Delicious, McIntosh, or Gala.

Green Grape Smoothie
(page 48)

3 | Green with Envy

If you've never tried a green smoothie before, now's the moment. Leafy greens fill a smoothie with chlorophyll, fiber, minerals, vitamins, and antioxidants that you can't get with just fruit. Go green, but keep it delicious with our Spicy Green Smoothie, Greens in a Glass, or Berry, Orange & Avocado Smoothie. If you're not a green guru, don't dive into kale right away—its bitter flavor may tempt you to add sugar. Milder-tasting spinach is a better choice. Once you've acquired a taste for greens, you're ready to branch out to kale. Soon afterwards you won't be tempted to share a drop!

Green Grape
SMOOTHIE

This blender wonder mixes celery, cucumber, grapes, and almond milk for a satisfying snack. For photo, see page 46.

TOTAL TIME: 5 MINUTES   **MAKES:** 2 SERVINGS (3 CUPS)

1½ cups sweetened almond milk

1   medium Kirby cucumber, peeled and sliced

1   cup green seedless grapes (preferably frozen)

2   medium stalks celery, peeled and sliced

2   teaspoons honey

In blender, combine almond milk, cucumber, grapes, celery, and honey and blend until mixture is smooth and frothy. Pour into 2 tall glasses.

EACH SERVING: ABOUT 145 CALORIES, 2G PROTEIN, 32G CARBOHYDRATE, 2G TOTAL FAT (0G SATURATED), 2G FIBER, 0MG CHOLESTEROL, 165MG SODIUM.

TIP

This recipe is also delicious with a handful of fresh mint, cilantro, or parsley leaves.

Fruity Green
SMOOTHIE

Talk about fully loaded with goodness! Five varieties of fruit, plus spinach, celery, and cucumber, makes this a truly super smoothie.

TOTAL TIME: 10 MINUTES   **MAKES:** 2 SERVINGS

2   cups water

½   cup baby spinach

2   stalks celery, chopped

1   Bartlett pear, cut up

1   green apple, cut up

1   ripe banana (preferably frozen), cut up

2   slices ripe mango

¼   cup diced pineapple

¼   English (seedless) cucumber, sliced

2   teaspoons honey

In blender, combine water, spinach, celery, pear, apple, banana, mango, pineapple, cucumber, and honey and blend until mixture is smooth and frothy. Pour into 2 tall glasses.

EACH SERVING: ABOUT 217 CALORIES, 3G PROTEIN, 53G CARBOHYDRATE, 1G TOTAL FAT (0G SATURATED), 9G FIBER, 0MG CHOLESTEROL, 46MG SODIUM.

Berry, Orange & Avocado
SMOOTHIE

This luscious smoothie gets a major green boost
from iron-rich spinach (the tender baby spinach leaves
keep the flavor naturally sweet).

TOTAL TIME: 10 MINUTES   **MAKES:** 4 SERVINGS

1   avocado

2½ cups orange juice

2   cups frozen mixed berries

2   cups packed baby spinach

2   cups ice cubes

In blender, combine avocado, orange juice, frozen berries, spinach, and ice and blend until mixture is smooth and frothy. Pour into 4 glasses.

EACH SERVING: ABOUT 183 CALORIES, 3G PROTEIN, 29G CARBOHYDRATE, 8G TOTAL FAT (1G SATURATED), 6G FIBER, 0MG CHOLESTEROL, 16MG SODIUM.

TIP

For a tasty twist, substitute baby kale for the spinach.

A is for Avocado Smoothies

Move over, guacamole, this luscious fruit is a "smooth" operator.

If a thick, luxurious green smoothie is what you seek, chances are it contains heart-healthy avocado. No surprise there, because like bananas, avocados are a fruit and share the same silky texture when blended. Avocados are extremely delicate (and perishable), so most are shipped to stores before they ripen. Nothing but a ripe avocado will do in a smoothie, so follow our crib sheet to ensure your green blend tastes like liquid gold. Bonus: Avocados are a good source of folate, fiber, and vitamin E.

TO SELECT

Look for the Hass variety, with pebbly skin that turns darker. Gently squeeze the fruit in the palm of your hand. A ripe, ready-to-eat avocado will feel firm but still yield to gentle pressure. (Avoid fruit with dark blemishes on the skin or overly-soft fruit.)

TO RIPEN

Place the fruit in a plain brown paper bag and store at room temperature for 2 days or until ready to eat. Add an apple or banana to the bag to speed up the process (these fruits give off natural ethylene gas, which will help ripen your avocados organically). Hint: The more apples or bananas you add, the quicker your avocados will ripen.

TO STORE

Soft ripe avocados can be refrigerated for at least 2 to 3 days.

Spicy Green SMOOTHIE

Jalapeño chile gives this all-veggie smoothie its zesty kick.

TOTAL TIME: 10 MINUTES **MAKES:** 1 SERVING

1¼ cups water

½ celery stalk, chopped

½ cucumber, sliced

¼ avocado

2 kale leaves

1 tablespoon chopped fresh cilantro

1 tablespoon lemon juice

¼ jalapeño chile with seeds

In blender, combine water, celery, cucumber, avocado, kale, cilantro, lemon juice, and jalapeño and blend until mixture is smooth and frothy. Pour into 1 tall glass.

EACH SERVING: ABOUT 104 CALORIES, 2G PROTEIN, 9G CARBOHYDRATE, 8G TOTAL FAT (1G SATURATED), 5G FIBER, 0MG CHOLESTEROL, 25MG SODIUM.

TIP

If you prefer your smoothie less spicy, remove the vein and seeds from the chile (as they are the hottest part of the pepper).

Greens
IN A GLASS

This smoothie is fully loaded with protein,
thanks to a single-serve container of Greek yogurt.

TOTAL TIME: 5 MINUTES **MAKES:** 1 SERVING

1 cup baby spinach

½ cup chopped cucumber

1 celery stalk, sliced

½ ripe banana, sliced

½ cup pineapple chunks

1 container (5.3 ounces) plain fat-free Greek yogurt

½ cup coconut water

4 ice cubes

In blender, combine spinach, cucumber, celery, banana, pineapple, yogurt, coconut water, and ice and blend until mixture is smooth and frothy. Pour into 1 tall glass.

EACH SERVING: ABOUT 223 CALORIES, 17G PROTEIN, 40G CARBOHYDRATE, 1G TOTAL FAT (0G SATURATED), 5G FIBER, 0MG CHOLESTEROL, 166MG SODIUM.

TIP

Use an English (seedless) cuke in this recipe.

Green Papaya
COOLER

Baby spinach and jalapeño provide the hue (and heat)
in this luscious smoothie. Frozen papaya chunks and cucumber
cool things off for pure refreshment.

TOTAL TIME: 5 MINUTES   **MAKES:** 1 SERVING

1   cup baby spinach

1   cup frozen papaya chunks

½   small cucumber, peeled and sliced

½   jalapeño chile, seeded

¼   cup coconut milk

In blender, combine spinach, papaya, cucumber, jalapeño, and coconut milk and blend until mixture is smooth and frothy. Pour into 1 glass.

EACH SERVING: ABOUT 194 CALORIES, 3G PROTEIN, 21G CARBOHYDRATE, 13G TOTAL FAT (11G SATURATED), 4G FIBER, 0MG CHOLESTEROL, 63MG SODIUM.

TIP

To prep the jalapeño, halve the chile lengthwise, and then use a melon baller or the tip of a grapefruit spoon to remove the seeds.

Creamy Kale
SMOOTHIE

Frozen pineapple chunks, fat-free milk, and Greek yogurt give this super K smoothie its creamy taste and texture.

TOTAL TIME: 5 MINUTES   **MAKES:** 1 SERVING

1   cup coarsely chopped kale

1½ cups frozen pineapple chunks

½   cup plain fat-free Greek yogurt

½   cup fat-free milk

1   teaspoon honey

1   teaspoon brown sugar

In blender, combine kale, pineapple, yogurt, milk, honey, and brown sugar and blend until mixture is smooth and frothy. Pour into 1 tall glass.

EACH SERVING: ABOUT 288 CALORIES, 17G PROTEIN, 58G CARBOHYDRATE, 0G TOTAL FAT, 5G FIBER, 2MG CHOLESTEROL, 102MG SODIUM.

TIP

Frozen pineapple chunks are available in convenient 1-pound bags at the supermarket. You can also substitute frozen mango chunks in this recipe.

Kale: The Latest Smoothie Fave

Kale is the "it" green veggie.

From curly to plain to dinosaur (Lacinato), kale has been popping up on restaurant menus all over the country. Delicious raw, this superfood, loaded with vitamins, antioxidants, and fiber, is now a smoothie staple as well. To get kale smoothie-ready, rinse, tear the gnarly leaves off (and discard) the tough stems, pile the leaves, and coarsely chop.

Tangy Mango Smoothie
(page 62)

4 Tropical Delights

There's something about the soothing flavor of tropical fruit that brings you close to smoothie paradise. And no wonder—the intense natural sweetness in fruits like mango, papaya, pineapple, and coconut make our smoothies like Tangy Mango, Healthy Piña Colada and Carrot-Pineapple exceptionally delicious, without the need for added sugar. Best of all, tropical fruits deliver generous portions of the vitamins you need. Not a bad payoff for going exotic.

Tangy Mango
SMOOTHIE

Low-fat buttermilk provides the tang in this creamy smoothie with ripe mango and a touch of spice. For photo, see page 60.

TOTAL TIME: 10 MINUTES **MAKES:** 1 SERVING (ABOUT 1¾ CUPS)

1   medium ripe mango (12 ounces), cubed

¾   cup buttermilk

4   ice cubes

1   teaspoon honey

¼   teaspoon vanilla extract

pinch ground cardamom or cinnamon, optional

In blender, combine mango, buttermilk, ice, honey, vanilla, and cardamom, if using, and blend until mixture is smooth and frothy. Pour into 1 tall glass.

EACH SERVING: ABOUT 272 CALORIES, 10G PROTEIN, 52G CARBOHYDRATE, 5G TOTAL FAT (3G SATURATED), 4G FIBER, 15MG CHOLESTEROL, 196MG SODIUM.

TIP

No buttermilk? Make your own! Place ¾ teaspoon lemon juice or white vinegar in a glass measure; add enough low-fat (1%) milk to equal ¾ cup. Stir; let stand 5 minutes.

Tropical Peach
SMOOTHIE

Fresh peaches, a good source of vitamins A and C,
combine with super-sweet mango for a tropical twist.

ACTIVE TIME: 15 MINUTES   **TOTAL TIME:** 20 MINUTES
MAKES: 2 SERVINGS

1   pound peaches, peeled and sliced

1   cup frozen mango or pineapple chunks

½   cup apple juice

½   cup vanilla low-fat yogurt

In blender, combine peaches, mango, apple juice, and yogurt and blend until mixture is smooth and frothy. Pour into 2 glasses.

EACH SERVING: ABOUT 208 CALORIES, 5G PROTEIN, 47G CARBOHYDRATE, 1G TOTAL FAT (0G SATURATED), 5G FIBER, 4MG CHOLESTEROL, 42MG SODIUM.

TIP

It's easy to peel fresh peaches! With a paring knife, score the pointed end of each peach in an **X** shape. Place 2 to 3 peaches in boiling water, 30 to 60 seconds, or until the skin begins to slightly pull away from the scored ends. With a slotted spoon, transfer the fruit to a bowl filled with ice water. Repeat. When the peaches are cool enough to handle, lightly pinch the softened skin and peel off with your fingers.

Tropic Thunder

Leave it to the tropics to produce fruits of exceptional health benefits to add to your smoothies.

PINEAPPLE not only tastes great with leafy greens, but it is also stocked with vitamin C, manganese, and copper. Vitamin C has diverse health benefits for our bodies, which makes it an important nutrient for overall health. Copper, though only needed in small amounts, helps those with anemia.

MANGO makes your smoothies extra creamy; plus they have lots of vitamins A and C, potassium, and fiber. Mangos are also a great substitute for bananas. Their soluble fiber helps bind the smoothies into a creamy consistency and naturally boosts the sweetness. Make sure you peel the skin and remove the seed before blending.

COCONUT is praised for its high amount of good cholesterol (HDL cholesterol), which decreases the risk of cardiovascular disease. Use coconut water or light coconut milk as a liquid base, a teaspoon of coconut oil as an added ingredient (and flavor boost), or even sprinkle coconut flakes for a burst of tropical flavor.

PAPAYA has a sweet and musky taste with soft, buttery flesh that will make your smoothie extra creamy. A good source of vitamin C and potassium, papaya also helps to digest protein with the enzyme papain.

KIWI is a sweet and tart fruit that will perk up your taste buds with shots of potassium, fiber, and vitamin C. Puree it with or without the skin.

Mighty Papaya
SMOOTHIE

Sweet mango and just a touch of honey
perfectly complement the earthy flavor of kale.

TOTAL TIME: 5 MINUTES   **MAKES:** 1 SERVING

1   cup frozen papaya chunks

1   cup coarsely chopped kale

½   cup vanilla fat-free Greek yogurt

½   cup fat-free milk

1   teaspoon honey

In blender, combine papaya, kale, yogurt, milk, and honey and blend until mixture is smooth and frothy. Pour into 1 tall glass.

EACH SERVING: ABOUT 233 CALORIES, 15G PROTEIN, 44G CARBOHYDRATE, 1G TOTAL FAT (0G SATURATED), 3G FIBER, 2MG CHOLESTEROL, 102MG SODIUM.

TIP

Whirl in a tablespoon of chia seeds for a nutritious boost.

Berry BATIDO

Batidos are the Latin American version of fruit smoothies.
We add walnuts to this recipe for a protein boost and subtle crunch.

TOTAL TIME: 5 MINUTES   **MAKES:** 1 SERVING

- 1 cup frozen strawberries
- 1 cup frozen blueberries or blackberries
- 1 cup raspberries
- 1 cup goji berries, optional
- 1 ripe banana, cut up
- 1 tablespoon walnuts, chopped

In blender, combine strawberries, blueberries, raspberries, goji berries (if using), banana, and walnuts and blend until mixture is smooth and frothy. Pour into 1 tall glass.

EACH SERVING: ABOUT 339 CALORIES, 6G PROTEIN, 73G CARBOHYDRATE, 7G TOTAL FAT (1G SATURATED), 19G FIBER, 0MG CHOLESTEROL, 5MG SODIUM.

TIP

Touted as an antioxidant powerhouse and high in vitamins C and E, goji berries are dried pink berries from the Himalayas and China. Their flavor is reminiscent of dried cranberries.

Healthy Piña Colada
SMOOTHIE

Pineapple and coconut milk give this smoothie
the classic taste you love. Serve in frosted glasses for brunch
with friends (see Get Frosted, page 73).

TOTAL TIME: 5 MINUTES   **MAKES:** 4 SERVINGS

1½ cups frozen pineapple chunks

1   ripe banana, cut up

1   can (14 ounces) light coconut milk

1   container (6 ounces) vanilla fat-free yogurt

½   cup ice cubes

In blender, combine pineapple, banana, coconut milk, yogurt, and ice and blend until mixture is smooth and frothy. Pour into 4 glasses.

EACH SERVING: ABOUT 173 CALORIES, 5G PROTEIN, 25G CARBOHYDRATE, 6G TOTAL FAT (6G SATURATED), 2G FIBER, 1MG CHOLESTEROL, 43MG SODIUM.

Piña Power!

Many smoothies (exotic or otherwise) start with a fruit
of succulent star quality, namely: pineapple.

While packaged frozen pineapple is convenient, imports from Costa Rica and other warm climates mean that fresh pineapple is widely available year round. So if you want to save some coin and go fresh, use our go-to guide:

- **Brown shell = ripe?** Not necessarily. Pineapple can be ready to eat even when the shell is green. Since the fruit won't continue to ripen after it has been picked, it's important that the pineapple is plump, with rounded shoulders and developed "eyes" that have filled out.

- **Go for green leaves and a firm shell.** Avoid fruit that is spongy, has dry or brown leaves, or has a sour aroma.

- **Buy it, freeze it.** Pineapple won't continue to ripen once picked. If not using right away, chill the whole fruit up to 4 days, then cut up and freeze.

Carrot-Pineapple
SMOOTHIE

Carrots get a tropical makeover in these luscious smoothies
with coconut milk, ginger, and pineapple.

TOTAL TIME: 10 MINUTES **MAKES:** 2 SERVINGS (2¼ CUPS)

1   cup unsweetened light coconut milk

1   cup frozen pineapple chunks

¾   cup freshly grated peeled carrot

¼   cup carrot juice

1   (½-inch) piece peeled fresh ginger, sliced

1   teaspoon agave nectar

grated carrot, for garnish

In blender, combine coconut milk, pineapple,
carrot, carrot juice, ginger, and agave and blend
until mixture is smooth and frothy. Pour into
2 tall glasses and garnish with grated carrot.

EACH SERVING: ABOUT 150 CALORIES, 3G PROTEIN,
20G CARBOHYDRATE, 7G TOTAL FAT (7G SATURATED),
3G FIBER, 0MG CHOLESTEROL, 40MG SODIUM.

TIP

If you can't find fresh carrot juice at the
supermarket, substitute with unsweetened
pineapple juice.

Creamy Kiwi
FREEZE

Newsflash! One kiwifruit provides more vitamin C than an orange—making this fizzy smoothie with frozen yogurt a healthful indulgence.

TOTAL TIME: 10 MINUTES   **MAKES:** 2 SERVINGS

2   kiwifruit, peeled and quartered

2/3   cup vanilla fat-free frozen yogurt

2/3   cup chilled sparkling water or club soda

2   teaspoons honey

In blender, combine kiwifruit, frozen yogurt, sparkling water, and honey and blend until mixture is smooth and frothy. Pour into 2 frosted glasses.

EACH SERVING: ABOUT 117 CALORIES, 3G PROTEIN, 27G CARBOHYDRATE, 0G TOTAL FAT, 2G FIBER, 3MG CHOLESTEROL, 56MG SODIUM.

TIP

To select kiwifruit, look for firm, unblemished fruit (don't worry about the size—smaller kiwifruit taste the same as larger ones). Press the outside of the fruit with your thumb. If it gives to slight pressure, the kiwifruit is ripe.

Get Frosted

To serve our Creamy Kiwi Freeze, opposite (or any of our smoothies) in a frosted glass, just follow these simple steps.

1 Place a small tray or rimmed baking sheet in the freezer.

2 Thoroughly rinse a clean glass with cold water and place immediately on the tray.

3 Repeat with additional glasses, allowing enough space in between for air to circulate.

4 Freeze for 1 to 2 hours or until the glasses are completely frosted.

Avocado & Kiwi
SMOOTHIE

Avocado makes this smoothie lusciously creamy, while
kiwifruit and pineapple add just the right amount of sweetness.

TOTAL TIME: 10 MINUTES   **MAKES:** 2 SERVINGS

1 avocado

2 kiwifruits, peeled and quartered

1 cup plain fat-free yogurt

1½ cups frozen pineapple chunks

In blender, combine avocado, kiwifruit, yogurt,
and pineapple and blend until mixture is smooth
and frothy. Pour into 2 tall glasses.

EACH SERVING: ABOUT 341 CALORIES, 11G PROTEIN,
46G CARBOHYDRATE, 15G TOTAL FAT (2G SATURATED),
11G FIBER, 2MG CHOLESTEROL, 103MG SODIUM.

TIP

To prep a kiwifruit with ease, slice the fruit
lengthwise in half and then use a spoon to
scoop out the flesh.

Red Strawberry Tea
(page 86)

5 Tea-riffic!

A glass of iced tea doesn't just offer pure refreshment—studies show it can do your body good. Tea is rich in a class of antioxidants called flavonoids, which are most potent when tea is freshly brewed. So it pays to skip the bottled stuff, and our Classic Iced Tea, Iced Fruit Tea, and Sun Tea show you how. For recipes that need to be chilled before serving, like our Red Strawberry Tea, add a squeeze of lemon or orange juice to the brew. The citric acid and vitamin C in the juice will help preserve the flavonoids.

Classic
ICED TEA

Use your favorite breakfast tea or fruit or herbal blend in this recipe.

ACTIVE TIME: 5 MINUTES   **TOTAL TIME:** 10 MINUTES PLUS STANDING
MAKES: 8 SERVINGS (ABOUT 8 CUPS)

8 black tea bags, tags removed

ice cubes

granulated or superfine sugar, optional

thin lemon slices, optional

1 In 3-quart saucepan, heat *4 cups cold water* to boiling over high heat. Add tea bags; remove from heat and cover. Let tea steep, 5 minutes.

2 Stir tea. Remove tea bags and pour brewed tea into 2½-quart pitcher with *4 cups cold water.* Cover and let stand until ready to serve. (Do not refrigerate or tea will become cloudy. If this happens, see Cloudy Tea? on opposite page.)

3 Fill 8 tall glasses with ice. Pour tea over ice and serve with sugar and lemon, if using.

EACH SERVING: ABOUT 2 CALORIES, 0G PROTEIN, 1G CARBOHYDRATE, 0G TOTAL FAT, 0G FIBER, 0MG CHOLESTEROL, 7MG SODIUM.

Cloudy Tea?

Does your home-brewed iced tea cloud after it's been refrigerated?
You're not alone.

When tea steeps, tannins—the natural compounds that color tea leaves—are released into the boiling water. The heat helps dissolve them, and the brew is clear enough to see through. But refrigeration causes tannins to separate out again, turning the tea murky. Here are some sure-fire ways to chase the clouds away:

- Generally, higher-quality tea contains more tannins (because it is richer in solids) and is more likely to become cloudy. Hard water is another culprit behind hazy tea.

- The Fix: stir ½ cup boiling water per gallon of iced tea just before serving, and voilà— clear tea. The extra water and rise in temperature are enough to blend the tannins back in.

- No time for boiling water? Use frosted glasses! (see Get Frosted, page 73.)

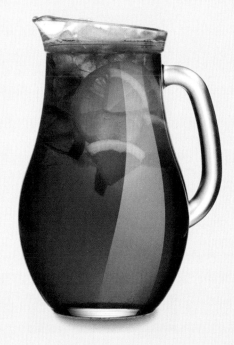

Iced Fruit TEA

This ultimate tea refresher is a blend of brewed tea
and your favorite fruit juice.

ACTIVE TIME: 5 MINUTES   **TOTAL TIME:** 10 MINUTES PLUS STANDING
MAKES: 8 SERVINGS (ABOUT 8 CUPS)

8   black tea bags, tags removed

4   cups unsweetened fruit juice (such as peach,
    cranberry, raspberry, or white grape)

ice cubes

fresh fruit, for garnish

1 In 3-quart saucepan, heat *4 cups cold water* to
boiling over high heat. Add tea bags; remove from
heat and cover. Let tea steep, 5 minutes.

2 Stir tea. Remove tea bags and pour brewed tea
into 2½-quart pitcher with fruit juice. Cover and
let stand until ready to serve. (Do not refrigerate
or tea will become cloudy. If this happens, see
Cloudy Tea? on page 79.)

3 Fill 8 tall glasses with ice. Pour tea over ice and
garnish with fruit, if you like.

....

EACH SERVING: ABOUT 38 CALORIES, 0G PROTEIN,
9G CARBOHYDRATE, 0G TOTAL FAT, 0G FIBER,
0MG CHOLESTEROL, 11MG SODIUM.

TIP

Summer berries are a perfect garnish
for this brisk beverage. Try raspberries,
blackberries, or a combination of the two.

Sun TEA

This refresher is ideal for those lazy, hazy days of summer because you don't even have to boil water—the sun does all the work for you.

ACTIVE TIME: 5 MINUTES   **TOTAL TIME:** 10 MINUTES PLUS STANDING
MAKES: 8 SERVINGS (ABOUT 8 CUPS)

8   tea bags, tags removed

ice cubes

granulated or superfine sugar, optional

thin lemon slices, optional

1   In large (2½-quart) glass jar or transparent container, stir together tea bags and *8 cups cold water*. Allow jar to stand in sun, covered, for 6 hours, or until strong tea is brewed.

2   Stir tea. Remove tea bags and pour brewed tea into 2½-quart pitcher. Cover and let stand until ready to serve. (Do not refrigerate or tea will become cloudy. If this happens see Cloudy Tea? on page 79.)

3   Fill 8 tall glasses with ice. Pour tea over ice and serve with sugar and lemon, if using.

EACH SERVING: ABOUT 2 CALORIES, 0G PROTEIN, 1G CARBOHYDRATE, 0G TOTAL FAT, 0G FIBER, 0MG CHOLESTEROL, 7MG SODIUM.

A Good Leaf

We'll help you get the most out of this bracing beverage.

Tea provides a modest dose of caffeine (about half the amount found in coffee), so it's the perfect middle ground if you're trying to limit your caffeine intake. Research also shows that tea (black, white, oolong, and especially green) contains cancer-fighting antioxidants and may also be linked to lessening anxiety.

- **Go for high-octane tea.** Health bonuses haven't been found as consistently in decaf versions.

- **Skip the dairy.** Adding milk to your tea concoction may blunt its heart-health benefits.

- **Keep it calorie-free.** Studies suggest that drinking unsweetened tea may help with weight management. Preliminary research suggests that tea flavonoids may help increase metabolism and fat oxidation and improve blood sugar control. Tea may also provide modest shifts in metabolism that may promote weight loss and maintenance.

Berry Tea
PICK-ME-UP

Tea gets the deluxe smoothie treatment in this creamy blend
with Greek yogurt, blueberries, and peaches.

ACTIVE TIME: 5 MINUTES   **TOTAL TIME:** 10 MINUTES PLUS COOLING
MAKES: 1 SERVING

- 1 cup brewed black tea, cooled to room temperature
- 1 container (5.3 ounces) vanilla fat-free Greek yogurt
- ½ cup frozen sliced peaches
- 1 cup fresh or frozen blueberries
- 5 to 10 ice cubes

In blender, combine brewed tea, yogurt, peaches, blueberries, and ice and blend until mixture is smooth and frothy. Pour into 1 tall glass.

EACH SERVING: ABOUT 218 CALORIES, 16G PROTEIN, 41G CARBOHYDRATE, 1G TOTAL FAT (0G SATURATED), 8G FIBER, 0MG CHOLESTEROL, 75MG SODIUM.

TIP

To quickly cool the brewed tea to room temperature, pour it into a small metal bowl and stick in the freezer. Freeze, stirring occasionally, for 5 to 10 minutes.

Red Strawberry TEA

This party-perfect refresher with fresh strawberries
is ideal for any summer gathering. For photo, see page 76.

ACTIVE TIME: 10 MINUTES   TOTAL TIME: 40 MINUTES PLUS STANDING AND CHILLING
MAKES: 12 SERVINGS

10 bags red tea, tags removed

1   pound strawberries, hulled and quartered

¼   cup sugar

2   cups pomegranate-cranberry juice blend

blueberry-topped skewers, for garnish

1 In 6-quart covered saucepot, heat *14 cups water* over high heat until almost boiling. Add tea bags; remove from heat and cover. Let tea steep, 10 minutes.

2 Remove tea bags and discard. Let cool slightly, then ladle some brewed tea into 1 ice cube tray. Freeze, uncovered, until solid. Pour remaining brewed tea into large punch bowl or pitcher. Refrigerate until very cold.

3 One hour before serving, in large bowl, combine strawberries and sugar. Let stand, uncovered, 30 minutes. Stir in juice blend, strawberries with accumulated juices, and tea ice cubes to tea mixture. Serve cold; garnish with skewers.

EACH SERVING: ABOUT 45 CALORIES, 0G PROTEIN, 11G CARBOHYDRATE, 0G TOTAL FAT, 1G FIBER, 0MG CHOLESTEROL, 5MG SODIUM.

TIP

To make ahead, prepare the recipe as directed through step 2 and chill up to 3 days.

Herbal Peach Tea
COOLER

This tea concoction is worthy of cocktail status
thanks to lemon-lime seltzer and fresh mint.

TOTAL TIME: 10 MINUTES PLUS COOLING   **MAKES:** 1 SERVING

1   peach herbal tea bag

ice cubes

¼   cup lemon-lime seltzer

1   mint sprig

1   In small glass measure, steep tea in *¾ cup boiling water*, 5 minutes; remove tea bag and cool to room temperature.

2   Fill 1 tall glass with ice. Pour brewed tea over ice. Add seltzer and garnish with mint sprig.

EACH SERVING: ABOUT 3 CALORIES, 0G PROTEIN, 1G CARBOHYDRATE, 0G TOTAL FAT, 0G FIBER, 0MG CHOLESTEROL, 4MG SODIUM.

TIP

This cooler is equally tasty with orange herbal tea.

TEA-RIFFIC!

Mango-Tea
DELIGHT

Green tea is delicious in a smoothie, and we give it a whirl
with vanilla Greek yogurt, succulent chunks of mango, and ice.

TOTAL TIME: 10 MINUTES PLUS COOLING   **MAKES:** 1 SERVING

1   green tea bag

½   cup vanilla fat-free Greek yogurt

1   cup fresh or frozen mango chunks

3 to 5 ice cubes

1 In small glass measure, steep tea in *½ cup boiling water*, 3 to 5 minutes; remove tea bag and cool to room temperature.

2 In blender, combine brewed tea, yogurt, mango, and ice and blend until mixture is smooth and frothy. Pour into 1 glass.

EACH SERVING: ABOUT 201 CALORIES, 11G PROTEIN, 40G CARBOHYDRATE, 1G TOTAL FAT (0G SATURATED), 3G FIBER, 0MG CHOLESTEROL, 37MG SODIUM.

Cranberry-Tea
REFRESHER

Green tea with ginseng gets a major buzz
with papaya, apple, and cranberry and grapefruit juices
for a smoothie that bursts with fruit flavor.

TOTAL TIME: 10 MINUTES PLUS COOLING   **MAKES:** 2 SERVINGS

½   cup chilled cranberry juice

½   cup chilled grapefruit juice

1   cup vanilla fat-free yogurt

½   papaya, seeded and cut up

½   red apple, cut up

½   cup brewed green tea with ginseng, cooled
to room temperature

5 to 7 ice cubes

In blender, combine cranberry juice, grapefruit
juice, yogurt, papaya, apple, brewed tea, and ice
and blend until mixture is smooth and frothy.
Pour into 2 glasses.

EACH SERVING: ABOUT 192 CALORIES, 6G PROTEIN,
41G CARBOHYDRATE, 0G TOTAL FAT, 2G FIBER,
3MG CHOLESTEROL, 98MG SODIUM.

TIP

Choose a papaya with reddish-orange skin
that's slightly soft to the touch. Fruit with
patches of yellow color will take a few days
to ripen.

TEA-RIFFIC!

Watermelon Slushie
(page 92)

6 | Spritzers, Slushies & Fizzes

A little icy, a little bubbly, and a whole bunch flavorful, these beverages will tantalize your taste buds while offering pure refreshment. Go bold and fruity with our Watermelon Slushie or Strawberry & Cucumber Slushie, or enjoy a healthful cocktail while you sip a Spiced Pomegranate Sparkler or Rosemary-Grapefruit Fizz. Our Citrus Spritzer is also perfect for a crowd. Any way you shake it, it's delicious.

Watermelon
SLUSHIE

With 2 cups of watermelon, this frosty drink contains excellent levels of vitamins A, B$_6$, and C, and also serves as a valuable source of potassium. For photo, see page 90.

TOTAL TIME: 5 MINUTES   **MAKES:** 1 SERVING (ABOUT 2 CUPS)

2   cups seedless watermelon, cut up into 1-inch pieces

½   cup pomegranate juice

½   cup ice cubes (about 4 large)

In blender, combine watermelon, pomegranate juice, and ice and blend until mixture is smooth. Pour into 1 tall glass.

EACH SERVING: ABOUT 170 CALORIES, 2G PROTEIN, 40G CARBOHYDRATE, 1G TOTAL FAT (0G SATURATED), 2G FIBER, 0MG CHOLESTEROL, 10MG SODIUM.

TIP

Choose a watermelon that is symmetrical, smooth, and heavy for its size. Turn it over; the underside should be yellow and the rind should have a healthy sheen. Ripe watermelon keeps up to 3 days in the fridge; wrap cut melon well to ward off refrigerator odors.

Spiced Pomegranate
SPARKLER

Cinnamon sticks and star anise give this pomegranate-and-cranberry refresher its harvest taste. Stir in fresh pomegranate seeds when in season.

TOTAL TIME: 15 MINUTES PLUS COOLING   **MAKES:** 2 SERVINGS

½   cup unsweetened cranberry juice

1   star anise

3   cinnamon sticks

1   cup pomegranate juice, chilled

1   cup sparkling water, chilled

ice cubes

2   lime wedges, for garnish

1   In small saucepan, heat cranberry juice, star anise, and 1 cinnamon stick to boiling over medium heat. Reduce heat to low; simmer 10 minutes. Cool. Discard spices.

2   Stir pomegranate juice and sparkling water into cranberry mixture. Fill 2 tall glasses with ice. Pour pomegranate mixture over ice and garnish with lime wedges and remaining 2 cinnamon sticks.

EACH SERVING: ABOUT 90 CALORIES, 0G PROTEIN, 22G CARBOHYDRATE, 0G TOTAL FAT, 0G FIBER, 0MG CHOLESTEROL, 10MG SODIUM.

TIP

No star anise? Substitute ¼ teaspoon of Chinese five-spice powder.

The Fizzes

Sparkling water, club soda, tonic . . . they all look the same.
But there's definitely a difference between the bubbles. Follow this guide
to make your next spritzer or fizz sparkle.

SPARKLING WATER (AKA: SELTZER)

WHAT Plain water + carbon dioxide

FLAVOR Very clean, often flavored with other ingredients like citrus; can be used
interchangeably with club soda.

. . . .

CLUB SODA

WHAT Plain water + sodium bicarbonate or potassium bicarbonate

FLAVOR Slightly more mineral-y tasting than sparkling water, but still a relatively
clean taste; can be used interchangeably with sparkling water.

. . . .

SPARKLING MINERAL WATER

WHAT Natural spring or well water (sometimes bottled at the source) + naturally
occurring carbonation and minerals

FLAVOR More delicate effervescence with distinct taste that can vary depending on
where the water came from; most expensive bubbly water, so best enjoyed solo.

. . . .

TONIC WATER

WHAT Plain water + carbon dioxide +
sweetener (usually corn syrup) + quinine

FLAVOR Sweet with slightly bitter
aftertaste; use only in recipes that
specify tonic.

Rosemary-Grapefruit
FIZZ

Fresh rosemary and a slice of lemon add just the right herbal
and citrus notes to this sophisticated fizz.

TOTAL TIME: 5 MINUTES   **MAKES:** 1 SERVING

⅔ **cup fresh red or pink grapefruit juice,
chilled**

⅓ **cup sparkling water, chilled**

1 **rosemary sprig**

1 **thin slice lemon**

Fill 1 tall glass with ice. Pour grapefruit juice over
ice. Add sparkling water and stir well. Garnish
with rosemary sprig and lemon slice.

EACH SERVING: ABOUT 66 CALORIES, 1G PROTEIN,
16G CARBOHYDRATE, 0G TOTAL FAT, 0G FIBER,
0MG CHOLESTEROL, 13MG SODIUM.

TIP

Rosemary packs a potent flavor punch, so
use a small sprig in this drink.

Cranberry & Lime FIZZ

This simple bubbly is sweetened with agave syrup.

TOTAL TIME: 5 MINUTES **MAKES:** 1 SERVING

ice cubes

¼ cup fresh lime juice

3 tablespoons unsweetened cranberry juice

½ teaspoon agave nectar

½ cup sparkling water, chilled

1 thin slice cucumber

1 Fill a cocktail shaker with ice. Add lime juice, cranberry juice, and agave; cover and shake until mixture is well combined.

2 Fill 1 tall glass with ice. Strain cranberry mixture over ice. Add sparkling water and garnish with cucumber slice.

EACH SERVING: ABOUT 48 CALORIES, 0G PROTEIN, 14G CARBOHYDRATE, 0G TOTAL FAT, 0G FIBER, 0MG CHOLESTEROL, 18MG SODIUM.

TIP

Before juicing citrus, roll it on the countertop to burst open some of the segments inside so it's easier to get at the juice. You'll need 2 limes for this recipe.

DIY Shaker

If you're lacking a cocktail shaker to prepare our healthful "mocktails,"
no worries—there are several alternatives you probably already own.

- **Mason or pasta sauce jar with lid.** Wash thoroughly, fill with ingredients and ice, close
  tightly, and shake. Holding lid slightly ajar, pour into glass.

- **Travel coffee mug.** Fill with ingredients and ice, screw on lid, and close drinking
  spout. Shake. Open drinking spout and pour into glass.

- **Empty milk or juice carton.** Wash thoroughly, fill with ingredients and ice, close
  tightly, and shake. Pour through small strainer into glass.

Lemony White Grape
COOLER

We shake up white grape juice, high in antioxidents
and vitamin C, with fresh lemon juice, a splash of brewed
chamomile tea, and a touch of honey.

TOTAL TIME: 5 MINUTES PLUS COOLING **MAKES:** 2 SERVINGS

½ **cup white grape juice**

½ **cup fresh lemon juice**

¼ **cup brewed chamomile tea, cooled
    to room temperature**

2 **teaspoons honey**

2 **lemon twists**

1 Fill cocktail shaker with ice. Add grape juice,
lemon juice, brewed tea, and honey; cover and
shake until mixture is well combined.

2 Strain grape juice mixture into 2 champagne
flutes and garnish with lemon twists.

EACH SERVING: ABOUT 70 CALORIES, 0G PROTEIN,
19G CARBOHYDRATE, 0G TOTAL FAT, 0G FIBER,
0MG CHOLESTEROL, 5MG SODIUM.

 TIP

To create our extra-fancy lemon twist,
cut the nubs from both ends of a lemon.
Holding a sharp paring knife at an angle
and starting at one end, remove the peel
(and some pith), working your way around
and down in an unbroken spiral. Rotate
the fruit, not the blade.

Pomegranate
SPRITZER

Drink up! Pomegranate is a deliciously sweet-tart member of the berry family that's rich in antioxidants, potassium, and vitamin C—plus, it's a great source of fiber.

TOTAL TIME: 5 MINUTES PLUS COOLING   **MAKES:** 1 SERVING

½ cup pomegranate juice

2 tablepoons fresh lemon juice

ice cubes

⅓ cup tonic water

5 pomegranate seeds

1 mint sprig

Fill 1 glass with ice. Pour pomegranate juice and lemon juice over ice and stir. Add tonic water and garnish with pomegranate seeds and mint sprig.

EACH SERVING: ABOUT 106 CALORIES, 1G PROTEIN, 27G CARBOHYDRATE, 0G TOTAL FAT, 0G FIBER, 0MG CHOLESTEROL, 25MG SODIUM.

TIP

Make your own pomegranate juice! Roll a medium pomegranate with the palm of your hand until the crackling stops (which indicates all the seeds are broken). Pierce the skin and squeeze out juice (you'll get about ½ cup). Hint: place the fruit in a plastic bag before rolling to catch any juice that may leak out through the skin.

Citrus SPRITZER

Looking for a thirst-quencher to serve a crowd?
Stir up our pitcher-ful of orange juice, lemon-lime seltzer,
sliced orange, and lime and serve it over ice.

ACTIVE TIME: 10 MINUTES   **TOTAL TIME:** 40 MINUTES
MAKES: 10 SERVINGS (ABOUT 10 CUPS)

4   cups orange juice

4   cups lemon-lime seltzer

2   oranges, sliced

2   limes, sliced

ice cubes

1   In large pitcher, stir together orange juice,
seltzer, orange slices, and lime slices. Refrigerate
until chilled, at least 30 minutes.
2   Fill 10 glasses with ice. Pour citrus mixture
over ice.

EACH SERVING: ABOUT 61 CALORIES, 1G PROTEIN,
15G CARBOHYDRATE, 0G TOTAL FAT, 1G FIBER,
0MG CHOLESTEROL, 4MG SODIUM.

TIP

If you have an extra-big crowd, make
another pitcher of spritzer with cranberry-
lime seltzer.

Strawberry & Cucumber
SLUSHIE

This delicious beverage with finely chopped ice
gets its kick from red zinger tea.

TOTAL TIME: 5 MINUTES PLUS COOLING   **MAKES:** 4 SERVINGS (ABOUT 6 CUPS)

- 2 cups brewed red tea (such as red zinger), cooled to room temperature
- 1 package (16 ounces) frozen strawberries
- ½ large English (seedless) cucumber, peeled and cut into 1-inch pieces
- 1 tablespoon sugar
- 2 cups ice cubes

In blender, combine brewed tea, strawberries, cucumber, sugar, and ice and pulse until mixture is finely chopped. Pour into 4 glasses.

EACH SERVING: ABOUT 57 CALORIES, 1G PROTEIN, 14G CARBOHYDRATE, 0G TOTAL FAT, 3G FIBER, 0MG CHOLESTEROL, 4MG SODIUM.

TIP

Have extra cantaloupe, honeydew, or watermelon? Freeze melon balls and use 2 cups instead of the ice in this recipe. You can also float them in any of our spritzers.

Tomato Soup with Shrimp
(page 108)

7 Soup's On

Blenders aren't only great for smoothies. This mighty machine also whips up terrific healthy soups. And thanks to lots of veggies, blender soups don't rely on typical fat-laden thickeners (i.e., butter and flour) either. Our healthful versions of classic chilled soups like Best-Ever Gazpacho and Chilled Cucumber Soup make a brilliant first course or satisfying snack. Plus, hot and hearty Ginger-Spiced Carrot Soup and Broccoli & Cheddar Soup offer easy main dish options that taste even better when prepared ahead. So dig in!

Tomato Soup
WITH SHRIMP

Nutrient-rich tomatoes (with loads of vitamin C and lycopene) and fresh basil star in a quick, cool dish topped with lean seared shrimp. For photo, see page 106.

ACTIVE TIME: 20 MINUTES   **TOTAL TIME:** 30 MINUTES
MAKES: 4 MAIN-DISH SERVINGS

- 3 pounds ripe tomatoes, cut into quarters
- ½ cup roasted red peppers
- ½ cup fresh basil leaves, chopped
- 3 cloves garlic, crushed with garlic press
- ½ teaspoon salt
- ground black pepper
- 5 ounces multigrain bread (about 4 slices), cut into ½-inch cubes
- 12 ounces shelled and deveined shrimp (16 to 20 count), sliced in half along back
- ¼ teaspoon dried oregano
- 1 tablespoon extra-virgin olive oil

1 Preheat oven to 400°F.

2 In blender, blend tomatoes, in batches if necessary, until very smooth. Return puree to blender, then add red peppers, half of basil, 1 clove garlic, salt, and ¼ teaspoon pepper; blend until smooth. Cover and refrigerate.

3 Prepare croutons: Arrange bread on jelly-roll pan. Bake 8 to 10 minutes or until golden brown, stirring once.

4 Meanwhile, in medium bowl, combine shrimp, oregano, remaining basil, remaining 2 cloves garlic, and ⅛ teaspoon pepper, tossing.

5 In 12-inch skillet, heat oil over medium-high heat until hot, but not smoking. Add shrimp; cook 4 to 5 minutes or just until shrimp turn opaque throughout, stirring occasionally. Divide soup and shrimp among 4 serving bowls; garnish with croutons and additional basil leaves.

EACH SERVING: ABOUT 255 CALORIES, 19G PROTEIN, 31G CARBOHYDRATE, 7G TOTAL FAT (1G SATURATED), 7G FIBER, 107MG CHOLESTEROL, 1,035MG SODIUM.

On the Ripe Side

Our Tomato Soup with Shrimp (left) and Best-Ever Gazpacho (page 110) rely on ripe tomatoes for best flavor. But if the only tomatoes you can find are not ready to eat, follow these steps to coax them into juicy readiness:

- **Store tomatoes at room temperature.** Refrigeration prevents ripening and kills flavor. A good spot is in your fruit bowl—where the presence of other fruit speeds up the process—or in a sealed brown paper bag, which traps ethylene gas, a natural ripening agent in all fruit.

- **Don't store tomatoes stem-side down, whether in a bowl or a bag.** The "rounded" shoulders are the most tender part and will bruise simply from the weight of the fruit.

- **Don't ripen tomatoes on a windowsill.** Direct sunlight softens them, but doesn't help to ripen.

- **Use ripe tomatoes within 2 to 3 days.** If you must refrigerate a fully-ripe tomato to prevent spoilage, let it come to room temperature before puréeing to bring out the best flavor.

- **Freeze ripe tomatoes if you have a surplus.** Rinse gently and pat completely dry. Then freeze whole in a freezer-weight, zip-tight plastic bag for up to 6 months. Use right from the freezer for soups and stews.

Best-Ever
GAZPACHO

Our update on the classic chilled soup from Spain combines ripe tomatoes with other favorite veggies from the garden. Add a splash of hot pepper sauce for extra zing.

TOTAL TIME: 30 MINUTES PLUS CHILLING   **MAKES:** 6 FIRST-COURSE SERVINGS (ABOUT 6½ CUPS)

2   medium cucumbers (about 8 ounces each), peeled and seeded

2   pounds ripe tomatoes (about 6 medium), seeded and chopped

½   medium red pepper, coarsely chopped

1   garlic clove, chopped

3   tablespoons fresh lemon juice

1   tablespoon olive oil

1   teaspoon salt

⅛   teaspoon coarsely ground black pepper

1   cup corn kernels from cobs (2 ears)

1   avocado, cut into ½-inch dice

¼   cup thinly sliced red onion

1 Cut 1 cucumber into ¼-inch dice; cut remaining cucumber into chunks.

2 In blender, in 2 batches, puree tomatoes, red pepper, garlic, lemon juice, oil, salt, black pepper, cucumber chunks, and *½ cup water*.

3 Pour tomato puree into large bowl; stir in diced cucumber. Cover and refrigerate until well chilled, at least 3 hours or overnight.

4 To serve, top soup with corn, avocado, and onion.

EACH SERVING: ABOUT 145 CALORIES, 3G PROTEIN, 19G CARBOHYDRATE, 8G TOTAL FAT (1G SATURATED), 5G FIBER, 0MG CHOLESTEROL, 470MG SODIUM.

Chilled Corn & Bacon
SOUP

Thick-cut bacon adds smokiness and Yukon gold potatoes bring buttery flavor to this creamy soup that only tastes indulgent.

ACTIVE TIME: 25 MINUTES   **TOTAL TIME:** 35 MINUTES PLUS CHILLING
MAKES: 8 FIRST-COURSE SERVINGS

4   slices thick-cut bacon, cut into ½-inch pieces

1   large shallot, finely chopped

3   cups corn kernels from cobs (about 6 ears)

1   large Yukon gold potato (8 ounces), peeled and shredded

⅛   teaspoon smoked paprika, plus additional for garnish

4   cups low-fat (1%) milk

⅛   teaspoon salt

⅛   teaspoon ground black pepper

¼   cup packed fresh cilantro leaves

1   In 12-inch skillet, cook bacon over medium heat, 6 to 8 minutes or until crisp and browned. With slotted spoon, transfer to paper towels to drain. If making ahead, cover and refrigerate the bacon overnight.

2   Drain and discard all but 1 tablespoon fat from skillet. Add shallots and cook over medium heat, 2 minutes or until golden and tender, stirring occasionally. Add 2½ cups corn, potato, and paprika. Cook 2 minutes, stirring, then add *⅔ cup water* and cook 7 minutes, or until liquid evaporates and vegetables are tender.

3   Remove skillet from heat and transfer corn mixture to blender. Add milk and salt and blend until mixture is very smooth. Cover and refrigerate until soup is very cold, at least 3 hours or overnight.

4   Divide soup among 8 serving bowls. Top with bacon, pepper, cilantro, and remaining ½ cup corn. Garnish with paprika.

EACH SERVING: ABOUT 188 CALORIES, 9G PROTEIN, 27G CARBOHYDRATE, 6G TOTAL FAT (3G SATURATED), 3G FIBER, 12MG CHOLESTEROL, 375MG SODIUM.

Off the Cob

Removing corn from the cob is as easy as 1-2-3!

1   Place an ear of corn in a large bowl or shallow roasting pan (this will keep the kernels from splattering).

2   Hold the ear firmly, stem-end down, and with a small, sharp knife, cut straight down the cob, two or three rows at a time, until all the kernels are removed.

3   Scrape the back of the knife blade down the cob to remove the corn "milk." (The "milk" is as tasty to add to soups as the kernels.)

Creamy Buttermilk-Beet
SOUP

This soup has just four basic ingredients—perfect
for when you're not in the mood to cook.

TOTAL TIME: 10 MINUTES   **MAKES:** 4 FIRST-COURSE SERVINGS (ABOUT 4 CUPS)

3 cups buttermilk

2 medium refrigerated cooked beets
   (about 12 ounces), sliced

½ teaspoon salt

1 tablespoon minced fresh dill

dill sprigs, optional

1 In blender, combine buttermilk, beets, and salt
and blend until very smooth. Stir in minced dill.

2 Divide soup among 4 serving bowls. Garnish
with dill sprigs, if you like.

EACH SERVING: ABOUT 95 CALORIES, 7G PROTEIN,
14G CARBOHYDRATE, 2G TOTAL FAT (1G SATURATED),
2G FIBER, 7MG CHOLESTEROL, 655MG SODIUM.

TIP

If not serving the soup right away, you can
refrigerate it in an airtight container for up
to 1 day.

Chilled Cucumber SOUP

Homemade curry oil adds a tropical flourish of flavor
to this summer classic.

ACTIVE TIME: 25 MINUTES **TOTAL TIME:** 30 MINUTES
MAKES: 4 FIRST-COURSE SERVINGS (ABOUT 4 CUPS)

CUCUMBER SOUP

- 2 English (seedless) cucumbers (about 12 ounces each), peeled
- 1 small garlic clove, crushed with garlic press
- 1 container (16 ounces) plain low-fat yogurt
- ½ cup low-fat (1%) milk
- 1 tablespoon fresh lemon juice
- 1¼ teaspoons salt

CURRY OIL

- 2 tablespoons olive oil
- ½ teaspoon curry powder
- ½ teaspoon ground cumin
- ¼ teaspoon crushed red pepper

GARNISH

- 1 small tomato, chopped
- 1 tablespoon sliced fresh mint leaves

1 **Prepare Cucumber Soup:** Cut enough cucumber into ¼-inch dice to equal ½ cup; reserve for garnish. Cut remaining cucumber into chunks. In blender, combine cucumber chunks, garlic, yogurt, milk, lemon juice, and salt and blend until almost smooth. Pour mixture into medium bowl; cover and refrigerate 2 hours or until cold.

2 **Prepare Curry Oil:** Meanwhile, in small saucepan, combine oil, curry powder, cumin, and crushed red pepper. Cook over low heat until fragrant and oil is hot, about 1 minute. Remove saucepan from heat; strain curry oil through sieve into cup.

3 **Prepare Garnish:** In small bowl, combine tomato and reserved diced cucumber.

4 Divide soup among 4 serving bowls. Spoon garnish into center of each serving; sprinkle with mint and drizzle with curry oil.

EACH SERVING: ABOUT 170 CALORIES, 8G PROTEIN, 15G CARBOHYDRATE, 9G TOTAL FAT (2G SATURATED), 2G FIBER, 8MG CHOLESTEROL, 830MG SODIUM.

Green Pea & Lettuce
SOUP

This emerald-green soup makes an elegant first course
for Easter dinner or any special occasion.

ACTIVE TIME: 5 MINUTES **TOTAL TIME:** 20 MINUTES
MAKES: 6 FIRST-COURSE SERVINGS (ABOUT 6 CUPS)

2 teaspoons olive oil

1 medium onion, finely chopped

1 can (14½ ounces) chicken broth

1 package (10 ounces) frozen peas

1 head Boston lettuce (about 10 ounces),
 coarsely chopped

¾ teaspoon salt

⅛ teaspoon freshly ground black pepper

⅛ teaspoon dried thyme

½ cup fat-free milk

1 tablespoon fresh lemon juice

mint sprigs, optional

1 In 4-quart saucepan, heat oil over medium heat. Add onion and cook, stirring occasionally, 5 minutes or until tender. Stir in broth, frozen peas, lettuce, salt, pepper, thyme, and *1 cup water*; heat to boiling over high heat. Reduce heat to low; simmer 5 minutes. Stir in milk.

2 In blender at low speed, with center part of cover removed to allow steam to escape, blend pea mixture in small batches until smooth. Pour soup into large bowl after each batch. Return soup to same saucepan. Heat through. Stir in lemon juice, and remove from heat.

3 Divide soup among 6 serving bowls. Garnish with mint sprigs, if you like.

EACH SERVING: ABOUT 75 CALORIES, 4G PROTEIN, 10G CARBOHYDRATE, 2G TOTAL FAT (0G SATURATED), 3G FIBER, 2MG CHOLESTEROL, 589MG SODIUM.

Ginger-Spiced Carrot
SOUP

Fresh ginger provides the kick, and carrots add a healthy dose
of beta carotene. Combined with brewed green tea,
this is a soothing soup the whole family will love.

ACTIVE TIME: 25 MINUTES   **TOTAL TIME:** 55 MINUTES
MAKES: 4 MAIN-DISH SERVINGS

4   green onions

4   slices fresh ginger, plus 1 teaspoon peeled
and grated fresh ginger

3   bags green tea, tags removed

1   tablespoon olive oil

1   medium onion, finely chopped

1½ pounds carrots, cut into ¾-inch-thick pieces

1   medium all-purpose potato, peeled and
chopped

½   teaspoon salt

¼   teaspoon freshly ground black pepper

2   cups frozen peas

1 From green onions, cut off white and pale
green parts; place in 5-quart saucepot. Thinly
slice green-onion greens; set aside.

2 To saucepot, add sliced ginger and *5 cups
water.* Heat to boiling over high heat. Add tea
bags. Cover; remove from heat. Let stand 10
minutes.

3 While tea steeps, in 12-inch skillet, heat oil
over medium-high heat. Add onion, carrots,
potato, ¼ teaspoon salt, and pepper. Cook 6
minutes or until golden, stirring. Add grated
ginger; cook 1 minute, stirring.

4 With slotted spoon, remove solids from pot,
squeezing liquid into pot; discard solids. Heat
liquid to boiling over high heat; stir in carrot
mixture. Reduce heat to maintain simmer. Cook
10 minutes or until vegetables are tender, stirring.

5 Transfer half of soup to blender; keep
remaining soup simmering. In blender at low
speed, with center part removed to allow steam
to escape, blend soup until very smooth. Return
pureed soup to pot. Stir in peas and remaining
¼ teaspoon salt. Cook 3 minutes or until peas are
bright green and hot. Divide soup among serving
bowls; garnish with sliced green onions.

EACH SERVING: ABOUT 205 CALORIES, 7G PROTEIN,
37G CARBOHYDRATE, 4G TOTAL FAT (1G SATURATED),
9G FIBER, 0MG CHOLESTEROL, 410MG SODIUM.

Broccoli & Cheddar
SOUP

Broccoli is a nutrient powerhouse: It's a great source
of vitamins K and C, folate, and potassium, in addition to being
high in fiber. And thanks to a few low-fat dairy substitutions,
this rendition of a comfort classic is superhealthy.

ACTIVE TIME: 35 MINUTES   **TOTAL TIME:** 1 HOUR
MAKES: 8 FIRST-COURSE SERVINGS (ABOUT 8 CUPS)

1   tablespoon olive oil

1   medium onion, chopped

¼   cup all-purpose flour

½   teaspoon salt

¼   teaspoon dried thyme

⅛   teaspoon ground nutmeg

¼   teaspoon coarsely ground black pepper

2   cups reduced-fat (2%) milk

1   can (14½ ounces) chicken broth

1   large bunch broccoli (1½ pounds), cut into 1-inch pieces (including stems)

6   ounces reduced-fat shredded sharp Cheddar cheese (1½ cups)

1   In 4-quart saucepan, heat oil over medium heat. Add onion and cook 10 minutes, stirring occasionally. Stir in flour, salt, thyme, nutmeg, and pepper; cook 2 minutes, stirring frequently.

2   Gradually stir in milk, chicken broth, and *1½ cups water*; add broccoli and heat to boiling over high heat. Reduce heat to low; cover and simmer until broccoli is tender, about 10 minutes.

3   In blender at low speed, with center part removed to allow steam to escape, blend broccoli mixture in small batches until very smooth. Pour puréed soup into large bowl after each batch.

4   Return soup to saucepan; heat to boiling over high heat, stirring occasionally. Remove saucepan from heat; stir in cheese until melted and smooth. Divide soup among 8 serving bowls.

EACH SERVING: ABOUT 159 CALORIES, 11G PROTEIN, 14G CARBOHYDRATE, 8G TOTAL FAT (4G SATURATED), 3G FIBER, 21MG CHOLESTEROL, 604MG SODIUM.

TIP

Garnish each serving of soup with an additional twist of freshly ground black pepper.

SOUP'S ON

Index

Photography Credits

Cover: iStock: ©habovka, ©Chiociolla (straws); back cover: depositphotos: ©olhaafanasieva

© James Baigrie: 27

© Chris Bain: 70

Corbis: © Lawton/SoFood: 116; © Magdalena Niemczyk: 73; © Studio R. Schmitz/the food passionates: 30

Deposit Photos: © Alekcey: 21; © belchonock: 109; © bergamont: 63; © cristi 180884: 15 (blackberries); © Dionisvera: 15 (raspberries & blueberries); © elenathewise: 89; © Fotosmurf: 18; © frantysek: 64; © karidesign: 43; © lspace: 93; ©kung_mangkorn: 39; © maxsol7: 79; © Pakynyushchyy: 34; © Pixels Away: 10 (chia seeds), 33; © Roxana: 15 (strawberries); © sailorr: 45, 64 (coconut); © satit_srihin: 64 (papaya); © urban_light: 49; © vkraskouski: 86; © xamtiw: 95

© Philip Friedman/Studio D: 7

Getty Images: © Alison Miksch: 83

© Brian Hagiwara: 11

© Hayley Harrison: 12

iStockphoto: © bit245: 57; © Chiociolla: 2 (straws); © Lachlan Currie: 64; © Floortje: 8; © fookphoto: 105; © GMVozd: 74; © habovka: 2; © Oliver Hoffmann: 52; © Jamesmcq24: 53 © jcnifoto: 24; © Kung_Mangkorn: 29; © m_speel: 96; © MarynaVoronova: 100; © merc67: 6, 67; © MosayMay: 60; © nata_vkusidey: 72, 119; © Lauri Patterson: 68; © PoppyB: 99; © Vitalina Rybakova: 16; © Sohadiszno: 10 (almond butter); © Spetnitskaya Nadya: 40; © Maartje van Caspel: 11; © victoriya89: 78; © Yasonya: 20, 64 (kiwi), 75; © zia_shusha: 115

© Kate Mathis: 23, 90, 106, 112, 120

© Michael Partenio: 76

Offset: © Leigh Beisch: 58

© Sarah Anne Ward/Studio D: 94, 100

Shutterstock: © Hurst Photo: 81; © Lecic: 85; © Mxhev: 122; © sarsmis: 103; © janecocoa: 97; © Julia Sudnitskaya: 36

Stock Food: © Foodografix: 46; © Deborah Ory: 51; © Magdalena Paluchowska: 54

Metric Conversion Charts

The recipes that appear in this cookbook use the standard United States method for measuring liquid and dry or solid ingredients (teaspoons, tablespoons, and cups). The information on this chart is provided to help cooks outside the U.S. successfully use these recipes. All equivalents are approximate.

METRIC EQUIVALENTS FOR DIFFERENT TYPES OF INGREDIENTS

STANDARD CUP	FINE POWDER *(e.g. flour)*	GRAIN *(e.g. rice)*	GRANULAR *(e.g. sugar)*	LIQUID SOLIDS *(e.g. butter)*	LIQUID *(e.g. milk)*
¾	105 g	113 g	143 g	150 g	180 ml
⅔	93 g	100 g	125 g	133 g	160 ml
½	70 g	75 g	95 g	100 g	120 ml
⅓	47 g	50 g	63 g	67 g	80 ml
¼	35 g	38 g	48 g	50 g	60 ml
⅛	18 g	19 g	24 g	25 g	30 ml

USEFUL EQUIVALENTS FOR LIQUID INGREDIENTS BY VOLUME

¼ tsp	=								1 ml
½ tsp	=								2 ml
1 tsp	=								5 ml
3 tsp	=	1 tbls	=			½ fl oz	=		15 ml
		2 tbls	=	⅛ cup	=	1 fl oz	=		30 ml
		4 tbls	=	¼ cup	=	2 fl oz	=		60 ml
		5⅓ tbls	=	⅓ cup	=	3 fl oz	=		80 ml
		8 tbls	=	½ cup	=	4 fl oz	=		120 ml
		10⅔ tbls	=	⅔ cup	=	5 fl oz	=		160 ml
		12 tbls	=	¾ cup	=	6 fl oz	=		180 ml
		16 tbls	=	1 cup	=	8 fl oz	=		240 ml
		1 pt	=	2 cups	=	16 fl oz	=		480 ml
		1 qt	=	4 cups	=	32 fl oz	=		960 ml
						33 fl oz	=		1000 ml = 1 L

USEFUL EQUIVALENTS FOR DRY INGREDIENTS BY WEIGHT

(To convert ounces to grams, multiply the number of ounces by 30.)

1 oz	=	1⁄16 lb	=	30 g
4 oz	=	¼ lb	=	120 g
8 oz	=	½ lb	=	240 g
12 oz	=	¾ lb	=	360 g
16 oz	=	1 lb	=	480 g

USEFUL EQUIVALENTS FOR COOKING/OVEN TEMPERATURES

	Fahrenheit	*Celsius*	*Gas Mark*
Freeze Water	32° F	0° C	
Room Temperature	68° F	20° C	
Boil Water	212° F	100° C	
Bake	325° F	160° C	3
	350° F	180° C	4
	375° F	190° C	5
	400° F	200° C	6
	425° F	220° C	7
	450° F	230° C	8
Broil			Grill

USEFUL EQUIVALENTS LENGTH

(To convert inches to centimeters, multiply the number of inches by 2.5.)

1 in	=					2.5 cm	
6 in	=	½ ft	=			15 cm	
12 in	=	1 ft	=			30 cm	
36 in	=	3 ft	=	1 yd	=	90 cm	
40 in	=					100 cm	= 1 m

THE GOOD HOUSEKEEPING
TRIPLE-TEST PROMISE

At *Good Housekeeping*, we want to make sure that every recipe we print works in any oven, with any brand of ingredient, no matter what. That's why, in our test kitchens at the **Good Housekeeping Research Institute**, we go all out: We test each recipe at least three times—and, often, several more times after that.

When a recipe is first developed, one member of our team prepares the dish, and we judge it on these criteria: It must be **delicious**, **family-friendly**, **healthy**, and **easy to make**.

1 The recipe is then tested several more times to fine-tune the flavor and ease of preparation, always by the same team member, using the same equipment.

2 Next, another team member follows the recipe as written, **varying the brands of ingredients** and **kinds of equipment**. Even the types of stoves we use are changed.

3 A third team member repeats the whole process **using yet another set of equipment** and **alternative ingredients**. By the time the recipes appear on these pages, they are guaranteed to work in any kitchen, including yours. **We promise**.